# prince ne

## Czarleen Ventura

BookLeaf
Publishing

India | USA | UK

prince neptune © 2024 Czarleen Ventura

All rights reserved.

Presentation by *BookLeaf Publishing*

Web: www.bookleafpub.com

E-mail: info@bookleafpub.com

ISBN: 9789358315356

First edition 2024

*to albus goldstein...*

*you made work bearable,*

*with those damn blue eyes.*

# ACKNOWLEDGEMENT

Thank you bookleaf publishing for this opportunity, I can't believe that I'm writing my fourth book, this has always been a dream of mine and, I can't believe that I'm living it.

Thank you jaycel, my dear bestfriend, you've always believed in me.
ate eunice, I miss you dearly, you're the first person who I send my poems to and, the first person I who update when I like someone.

Hello ate tamerlane, for the support and, also for the wake up calls for my delusional self. I agree that prince neptune does look like Jesus Christ. You're the only person who witnessed everything lol.

Thank you my beautiful readers, I hope you enjoy my art. I sincerely appreciate it.

# PREFACE

prince neptune, also called albus goldstein-
not his real name-
he is mysterious-
he keeps his secrets in a treasure chest;
I told tales about his golden heart;
I tried to translate it into different-
forms of art;
he will leave-
but, the poetry will live on-
in my silver life;
he was a metaphor;
a metaphor
I waited to write about my whole life.

# seafoam green

have you ever been lost into someone's eyes?
like drowning in the deepest trench,
except when I gazed at them, one slow second;

they were seafoam green,
like when the sun made the shore glisten;
back home in palawan-
appearing like perfect marbled glass;

inviting you to douse;
maybe, that's how wanderers end up missing;
swimming into the ocean named you;

- A nautical reference while residing in the
countryside,
I wonder what you look like under the sunlight?
like a crystal green orb with a heart of gold;

there's a first to every little thing;
I've never been a fan of blue eyes;
but, his gaze makes me want to dive.

# summertime

He is summertime-
-in a place of gloom and forlorn;
you're like a drop of starlight;
you're down to earth,
but, you're otherworldly;
the last one was beautiful;
but, you're surreal.

# teal

I was playing around the color wheel;
trying to understand how I feel;
how could this happen?

how can he not try at all?
and look like the image of the sea;
so captivating, his soul screams the color teal.

# random words

Fireworks, butterflies, hearts, sparks, random
words,
- I fell again like it's the first,
- And, I'm going to do it like it's my last.

for a small framed girl to feel too much,
I cannot deny the truth, evidenced by the flush;
when he looked at me, It feels like getting
washed out by the flood.

he's like a body of water with waves so strong;
his entrance was impactful, left me with a crush.

neptunian, thalassic, gorgeous, calm;

random words, you're like a trophy;
a shining star; boy, you're so pretty;
unreachable by my palms.

# the letter that I sent

my impulsiveness is both a curse and a blessing;
maybe witchcraft can end with a fairytale
ending;
I haven't met him before;
my letter's recipient;
that way it's memorable-
but, easy to forget;
someone who isn't implanted yet,
will he reply?
to the very first letter that I sent.

# sequined

I was walking the streets of soho,
right after doing something that I never thought
so,
all the men looked fine in their business suits,
but, you shine in scrubs alone,
apple green lanyard,
forest green shoes,
that's the sequined truth.

# thalassic eyed

thalassic eyes, your character gleams,
the heat was as cruel as the secret I'm keeping;
when he smiles; the constellations shy;
and, he doesn't really know it;
If darling is a sin;
then I will commit it;
to wake up to your gaze,
infinitely touch your face;
tell me pretty lies;
while I drown in your thalassic eyes.

# sparklers

you're like a daydream
under the midnight sky,
royal blue with fireworks
clearing up high;

A work of art;
forbidden to have printmarks;
salt water drunk on blue green tiles;

I love it when you smile;
you're a gallery at the beachside;
you make sparklers fill up the sky.

# golden

products from street art,
pastel colored chalk dust,
shadows from the beacon light;
disperse as glitter in the wind;

I look at him like I've never been-
enchanted before;
attracting mystical sirens
swim to his shore;

the boats are sinking;
the men are dreaming;
what's it like to be like him?
golden and classic.

# painting

he's a painting of the sea,
walking with a golden frame,
I'm an archer who's about to aim;
I loved enough to recognize the flame;

manifesting is not enough;
In silence I exclaimed;
I'll write you poetry;
the words will be famed;

If I get lucky;
they'll speak of our love's name;
you're a center piece;
In a museum at thames;

you're a painting of the crystalline sea-
with a golden frame.

# Love,Love

I love the feeling of falling over a body of pastel
clouds;
I love it when my insides spark like fireworks
without a sound.
I love it when I can't stop smiling like a jester
clown;
falling in love is one of my favorite things;
as if all the heartache doesn't fucking sting.
the beginning is the most magical of all;
the surrender of my castle guards during the fall;
that everytime it happens;
I want to scream at the top of my lungs,
retching as it's enchanting;
I'm in love with the feeling.
Love,love.

# impulse

hair dye, random walks at midnight;
fast food even though I'm broke,
my poetry is spontaneous;
I never understood why;
amidst my anxiety;

I write to speak my mind;
some days, I'm gentle petal sleeves;
sometimes, a chaotic planetarium dream;
I never understood why;
my impulses flood;
leaving deserts dry.

# you look like...

you look like a summer day;
covered with blue-green haze;
reflecting crystals;
in lieu with the teal sky;
and sunlight hues;
words fictional;
you look like a mistake I made;
writing on paper airplanes;
sacred texts; can't be erased;
you look like my wildest dreams;
a mirage of hopeless wishes;
an unanswered prayer;
you look like a mishap-
in my series of star lights;
passing through my auroras;
you look like the shore-
the view from the beach house;
you hit me like a raging tsunami;
you look like someone-
who I can spend forever living for-
at the same time ruined for.

# to my muse

to my muse;
it's not your fault;
a poet fancied you;
do not be afraid of the hurt;

for I didn't mean to enter-
your unruffled world;
but, know this;
I meant every word.

# give me my brain back...

the summer that I lost my brain;
it's like planet earth physically exploded;
that's how it felt.

more than a fluttering heart or a skipping beat,
I lost my brain-
will you kindly give it back?

I swear I'm a smart person-
I'm stupid when I'm in love;
give me my brain back...

# prussian blue ( how I felt about you )

at first sight;
they were seafoam green;
like when the shore is hit by sunlight;
as I gaze into his eyes;
I realized; they were prussian blue-
all this damn time;
and, the depth of the ocean-
is the metaphor of how I feel about you;
it went from pastel crystalline green-
to deep pigmented blue.

# the girl with the purple notes

can you atleast not forget about me?
if this was a game, I will call a forfeit;
for it's already unfair;
that the next opportunity-
that you receive your mail;
you'll snicker and flashback-
to the day that you found out.
that wherever you go;
you'll remember the girl with the purple notes-
and,rainbow hair.

to be born like that-
Is just fucking unfair.

# It's been waiting for you

it's been waiting for you;
the pages and the ink-
laid out on the table;
waiting for the right words;
waiting for the right muse.
everybody knows;
my face couldn't lie;
I tell them you're in my heart;
but, you're more than that;
you're the words in my poetry;
the poetry in my notebook;
the lyrics to my songs;
the inspiration in my paintings.

it's been waiting for you;
the artist in me.

# same admiring eyes

the day I realized that I'm in too deep;
there's no turning back;
it's the horrible aftermath;
I can still feel the wave shocks;
you wore the same baby blue tunic;
it felt like day one;
I'm going to write about it;
I sped home and, binged write;

you're still kind and steadfast;
you still have the same glimmer-
with that goddamn smile;
impactful as a passerby;
it feels too infinite;
that even if I reach the last page;
I will still look at you-
with the same admiring eyes.

# clone

you have a new clone in town;
you have the same eyes and smile;
haven't you figured out?
after all this time;
you will see my poems;
when you cross the road;
from a bookshop-
back in darlington;
you have a new clone in town;
you both laugh at my jokes;
when I make you grin;
it makes me frown;
you have a new clone in town;
you're way too similar;
charming prince like character;
and, you both have a girl down south.
I have nothing but my poetry;
and, my magical mind;
I just can't unsee this-
the resemblance is uncanny-
with your new clone in town.

# forever and always

hello, it's me from day one;
you wouldn't know-
because, to you it was a day;
to me, it was the day;

I haven't seen you in forever;
whenever I see you;
I remember the whys and hows;
you shine like a beacon-
in a lighthouse;

I had one last look-
at your saltwater eyes;
it made me forget-
the lengthy time;

I haven't seen you in forever;
the days swiftly passed;
you were the one-
I never had;

in a century;
will I be the same?
will it always feel like day one?
you will always be the one-

that I want;

somehow, it feels like
after a milenium-
the answer will always be yes;
forever and always;
I will always feel the same.

Milton Keynes UK
Ingram Content Group UK Ltd.
UKHW022336050624
443649UK00018BA/1091

9 789358 315356